Philadelphia 76ers

Michael E. Goodman

CREATIVE EDUCATION

Published by Creative Education
123 South Broad Street, Mankato, Minnesota 56001
Creative Education is an imprint of The Creative Company

Designed by Rita Marshall

Photos by: Allsport Photography, Associated Press/Wide World Photos,
Focus on Sports, NBA Photos, UPI/Corbis-Bettmann, and SportsChrome.

Photo page 1: Julius Erving
Photo title page: Jerry Stackhouse

Library of Congress Cataloging-in-Publication Data

Goodman, Michael E.
Philadelphia 76ers / Michael E. Goodman.
p. cm. — (NBA today)
Summary: Highlights the players, coaches, playing strategies, and
memorable games in the history of the Philadelphia 76ers basketball team.
ISBN 0-88682-886-4
1. Philadelphia 76ers (Basketball team)—Juvenile literature.
[1. Philadelphia 76ers (Basketball team)—History. 2. Basketball—History.]
I. Title. II. Series: NBA today (Mankato, Minn.)

GV885.52.P45G66 1997   96-51067
796.323'64'0974811—dc21

First edition

5 4 3 2 1

Philadelphia is a Greek word that means "City of Brotherly Love." But former President John F. Kennedy had
his own way of describing Philadelphia, Pennsylvania. He
called the historic city on the Delaware River "our nation's
hero factory." Philadelphia is where the Declaration of Inde-
pendence was signed by America's founding fathers; where
Benjamin Franklin established the country's first public library and first newspaper; where Betsy Ross sewed the first
American flag; and where Edgar Allan Poe created some of
America's best-loved poems and stories. The Philadelphia
"hero factory" has also produced its share of sports greats

who have brought many championships to the city's professional franchises—the baseball Phillies, football Eagles, hockey Flyers, and basketball 76ers. Of these Philadelphia teams, none has produced more local and national heroes than the 76ers. From the team's founding in 1963 until today, such Sixers stars as Dolph Schayes, Wilt Chamberlain, Hal Greer, Billy Cunningham, Julius Erving, George McGinnis, Moses Malone, Maurice Cheeks, Charles Barkley, Jerry Stackhouse and Allen Iverson have delivered excitement and excellence to basketball fans and have helped create a winning tradition in Philadelphia.

1 9 5 1

Dolph Schayes, the NBA's rebounding leader, was in the top 10 in both scoring and assists.

A TEAM LOST, A TEAM GAINED

The history of pro basketball in Philadelphia began not with the 76ers, but with another team known as the Warriors. The Warriors were an original member of the Basketball Association of America (BAA), formed in 1946. They won the league's first championship. When the BAA merged with another league in 1949 to form the National Basketball Association (NBA), the Philadelphia Warriors became a charter member of the NBA as well.

During the early years of the NBA, one of the teams the Warriors battled in the league's Eastern Division was a club from Syracuse, New York, called the Nationals, or Nats. Little did Philadelphia fans realize that, in 1962, the Warriors would decide to pack their bags and move to San Francisco, and the Nats would establish a new life the next year in the City of Brotherly Love.

The Nats team that moved to Philadelphia in 1963 had

Explosive forward Clarence Weatherspoon.

Guard Hal Greer earned his first of seven consecutive berths on the All-NBA team.

two future Hall of Famers: a high-scoring guard named Hal Greer and a basketball legend named Dolph Schayes, who was nearing the end of his career. Both made their mark in Philadelphia as well.

During his 16-year career in Syracuse and Philadelphia, Schayes was named to the NBA All-Star team 12 times and to the All-NBA first team six times. During one stretch, he established a league record by starting in 706 consecutive games. "It's an amazing statistic," marveled basketball historian Michael Allpress, "and a tribute to the human spirit when one considers the pounding Schayes took in a typical game. Because he was the kind of man who refused to relinquish so much as an inch under the boards, he emerged from most games with his upper body bright with red welts."

The secret to Schayes's durability was great determination and conditioning. "I didn't have much speed, but I felt that by constantly moving I could free myself, so I moved in and out all during the game. I kept pushing myself. I saw myself never getting tired. I was perpetual motion on the court. A couple of players called me 'The Circler' because I constantly circled around and made figure eights."

When the Nats moved to Philadelphia and changed their nickname to the 76ers, the obvious choice for the club's first coach was Dolph Schayes. He served as a player/coach during the 1963–64 season and then retired as a player so he could devote his full time to coaching the 76ers the next two years. All three years, the Sixers made the playoffs. In Schayes's final season as coach, the club won 55 games to lead the NBA's Eastern Division, and Schayes was named NBA Coach of the Year.

During his first season at the helm, Schayes relied heavily on his longtime teammate Hal Greer to handle much of the team's scoring and ball handling. Greer was an outstanding jump shooter who was deadly accurate between 15 and 20 feet from the basket. Even when he took free throws, Greer jumped before releasing the ball. In 1963–64, Greer led the new Philadelphia club in every offensive category except rebounding, which was the domain of veteran center Johnny Kerr and second-year forward Chet Walker.

1 9 6 4

Johnny Kerr hit the 1,000 rebound mark for the third year in a row.

Sixers management was happy with the new club's progress during its first season in Philadelphia, but it wanted more. The Sixers hoped to establish a championship club right away, and they thought the man who could turn the team into a big winner immediately was a native Philadelphian named Wilt Chamberlain. So, in a blockbuster move in January 1965, the Sixers sent three players and a large sum of money to the San Francisco Warriors in exchange for Chamberlain.

THE "BIG DIPPER" COMES HOME

P hiladelphia fans knew all about Wilt Chamberlain, even before he arrived to become the 76ers' "savior." Some called the 7-foot-1 Chamberlain "Wilt the Stilt," a nickname that usually brought a scowl to the big guy's face. Chamberlain much preferred being called "Big Dipper," a name that his old teammates at Philadelphia's Overbrook High School had originally given him. During his high school career, Chamberlain amassed more than 2,250 points. Then he headed to the University of Kansas, where he led his team,

Hall of Famer Hal Greer.

The legendary Wilt Chamberlain.

the Jayhawks, all the way to the NCAA finals. Following two seasons at Kansas, Chamberlain spent several years traveling the world with the Harlem Globetrotters.

In 1959, Chamberlain decided to turn pro, and the hometown Philadelphia Warriors were quick to sign him up. He immediately established himself as the greatest offensive performer in the history of the NBA. During his third season with the Warriors, 1961–62, Chamberlain dipped, stuffed, and soared his way to these amazing statistics: a scoring average of 50.4 points per game, a rebounding average of 27.2 per game, and a minutes-played average of 48.5 per game (including several overtime contests).

Philadelphia fans both loved and hated Wilt Chamberlain. They marveled at his offensive skills, but they also wondered why he could never lead the Warriors to a championship. Wilt

All-Star Larry Costello (21) led the 76ers with an 87.7 free-throw percentage.

Record-setting great Wilt Chamberlain.

and the Warriors always seemed to come in second best to Bill Russell and the Boston Celtics. Warrior fans grumbled that Wilt shot too much. They said he should learn to be more like Russell, to pass more and to play better defense.

The criticism puzzled Chamberlain. "If I don't score a lot of points," he said, "the fans are disappointed. But when I do score a lot of points, they call me a one-dimensional player."

Nevertheless, the Philly fans were sad to see Chamberlain and the Warriors leave when the club moved to San Francisco in 1962. And they were ecstatic when the Big Dipper came back home in 1965.

With Chamberlain in the lineup, backed by Greer, Chet Walker, and Luke Jackson, and coached by Dolph Schayes, the Sixers were transformed from a .500 team to a tough championship contender. The club reached the Eastern Division finals in both 1965 and 1966, only to fall each time to Bill Russell's Celtics. Yet it seemed clear that the Sixers' day on top would soon come.

Following the 1966 playoffs, Dolph Schayes decided to retire as coach and pass the team's reins to Alex Hannum. "I feel I have accomplished what I set out to do here in Philadelphia," said Schayes in his farewell address to the Sixers' fans. "I have every reason to believe that this team can be the next world champions." Schayes would turn out to be a prophet.

1 9 6 6

Billy Cunningham averaged 14.3 points per game and earned NBA All-Rookie honors.

CHAMBERLAIN + CUNNINGHAM = CHAMPIONSHIP

One of Dolph Schayes's last important moves as coach was to draft a young forward named Billy Cunningham out of the University of North Carolina. Nicknamed the

Wally Jones led the club in free-throw percentage (83.8) for the first of four consecutive years.

"Kangaroo Kid" for his jumping ability and aggressiveness, Cunningham brought new fire to the 76ers lineup. He also took some of the scoring and rebounding pressure off Chamberlain, so that Chamberlain could focus his energy on defense and passing. He was no longer a one-dimensional scoring machine but instead became an all-purpose threat.

When Alex Hannum took over as coach before the 1966–67 season, the team assembled before him included Chamberlain, Cunningham, Greer, Walker, and point guard Wally Jones, acquired in a trade with Baltimore. It was an awesome crew. The club won 45 of its first 49 games and finished with a 68–13 record, the fourth best in NBA history. Nor did the 76ers stop there. They defeated Cincinnati 3–1 in the opening round of the playoffs, demolished Boston 4–1 in the Eastern Division finals, and wrapped up the NBA championship with a 4–2 trouncing of Chamberlain's old team, the San Francisco Warriors. The "Big Dipper" finally had his championship. It was a sweet victory, but, unfortunately, it was short-lived.

A DOWNWARD SPIRAL

The 76ers began the 1967–68 season as if their championship year had never ended. Nearly all of their players were back again and raring for another title. By season's end, the Sixers' 62–20 record had them eight games ahead of the second-place Celtics. The experts assumed the Sixers were destined to repeat as world champs. Supposedly, the aging Celtics were over the hill.

By game five of the Eastern Division finals against Boston,

Eleven-time All-Star Julius Erving.

the Sixers seemed confident, and why not? After all, they had won three of the first four games and needed only one more victory to eliminate Boston. No team had ever come back after being down three games to one in a playoff series.

Then the seemingly impossible occurred. In an effort to psyche up his team, Boston's longtime coach Red Auerbach announced that he was retiring after the playoffs, and that Bill Russell would be his replacement. The announcement gave new life to the Celtics. Boston wiped out the Sixers in three straight contests and then roared past the Lakers for its 10th championship in 12 years. The 76ers were crushed and demoralized by their unexpected defeat.

The loss triggered a chain of events that ultimately sent the Sixers into a terrible downward spiral. First, Alex Hannum resigned as coach following the 1968 playoffs to move to the newly formed American Basketball Association (ABA). Next, Wilt Chamberlain expressed discontent with Philadelphia and was traded to Los Angeles for cash and three players.

Jack Ramsay, who had served as the Sixers' general manager for three years, was named Philadelphia's new head coach. Though Ramsay led the team to a second-place finish in the East in 1968–69, they fell to Boston in the first round of the playoffs. The situation would only get worse.

Over the next six seasons, the once-mighty 76ers won only 187 games and lost 305. The 1972–73 season was the most upsetting of all. Billy Cunningham, who had become the heart of the team after the Chamberlain trade, jumped ship to the ABA. That same year, the Sixers went through two coaching changes. Both men, Roy Rubin and Kevin Loughery, were inexperienced. At one point, the team lost

20 games in a row. They finished with a humiliating 9–73 record, the worst percentage in NBA history.

ENTER "BIG GEORGE," "THE DOCTOR," AND "BJ"

The 76ers franchise had sunk to the lowest point in its existence. For three straight years, Philadelphia was stuck in the Eastern Division cellar. The club's lineup consisted mainly of aging veterans and journeymen, with only one legitimate scoring threat—a speedy guard named Fred Carter, whose reckless play earned him the nickname "Mad Dog." Immediate help was desperately needed to rejuvenate the once-proud team.

That assistance arrived in three stages, starting with the 1975–76 season. All three players who helped turn the club around began their careers in the ABA. First to arrive on the scene was power forward George McGinnis, who jumped from the ABA Indiana Pacers to the Sixers before the 1975–76 season. McGinnis was a 6-foot-8 muscle man with a special talent for getting offensive rebounds and putting the ball back in for easy hoops. For a man of his size, he was amazingly quick. He had been voted co-MVP of the ABA in 1974–75, but some experts wondered if he could succeed against the tougher NBA competition. No one doubted "Big George" after his first year in Philadelphia, however. McGinnis led the club in scoring, rebounding, and steals that season and was second in assists and blocked shots. He was also named to the All-NBA first team.

A year later, the Sixers made an even more impressive acquisition. On October 21, 1976, word reached the city of

1 9 7 1

Fred Carter pulled down 485 rebounds and missed only one game of the season.

MVP Moses Malone (pages 18–19).

At 18, Darryl Dawkins was the first player drafted into the NBA directly out of high school.

Philadelphia that the financially troubled New Jersey Nets had sold the high-priced contract of 26-year-old Julius "Dr. J" Erving to the 76ers. Erving, the man of a thousand moves and soaring dunks, began an 11-year career in Philadelphia that would send the Sixers soaring as well. During that period, the Sixers never had a losing record. "Dr. J is a once-in-a-lifetime player," said 76ers general manager Pat Williams.

During his first six seasons in the ABA, Erving had been the class of that league, both as a player and as a man. "There are athletes who are known as 'the franchise,'" said Dave DeBusschere, the ABA commissioner who had starred on two NBA championship teams in New York, "but Julius isn't the franchise—he's the league."

Once he arrived in the NBA with the Sixers, Erving maintained his high level of play and sportsmanship. Summing up his philosophy of life and basketball, Erving said, "Whatever formula you apply to your life should be the one that enables you to maintain consistency, and I'm kind of a fiend about consistency. On the court I try to stay away from peaks and valleys. People have paid to see me perform. I perform and want to do well for them, but also for myself, for my own pride and desire."

With Julius Erving joining George McGinnis on the Sixers' front line, many people thought Philadelphia would be guaranteed a championship in 1976–77. But those expectations were not realized. The 76ers won the Atlantic Division, beat Boston in the conference semifinals, and then downed Houston to win the Eastern Conference crown. But it was the Portland Trail Blazers and Bill Walton who proved more consistent in the NBA finals.

After the 1977–78 season got off to a lackluster start for Philadelphia, coach Gene Shue was fired and replaced by former 76ers star Billy Cunningham. Cunningham quickly turned the club around, and it finished the season with a 55–27 record, its best in a decade.

Cunningham believed in a team concept that stressed balanced play at all positions, and he looked for great team players. When he traded George McGinnis to Denver for Bobby Jones before the 1978–79 season, Cunningham brought the ultimate team player to Philadelphia. "BJ" was one of the finest defensive forwards in NBA history. For 10 straight seasons (eight of them with the 76ers), Jones was elected to the NBA's first team All-Defensive squad. He could have been a fine scorer, but chose instead to concentrate on the other, less heroic aspects of the game. When asked to describe an ideal game for him, Jones replied, "Five offensive rebounds, five defensive rebounds, 10 assists, five blocked shots, five steals, and no turnovers in 25 minutes." Billy Cunningham loved that kind of unselfishness.

George McGinnis averaged more than 14 points and 10 rebounds per game during the NBA playoffs.

Cunningham found another great team player in the 1978 college draft, a 6-foot-3 guard from West Texas State named Maurice Cheeks. Cunningham made Cheeks his floor general, the man who would control the ball and make sure it was distributed to the right people in the right places to score. "Billy always knew that with Maurice in charge, he never had anything to worry about," said former NBA coach Dave Wohl. "Mo was an extension of Billy's thought on the floor."

Billy Cunningham's Philadelphia squads of the late 1970s and early 1980s—featuring such players as Erving and Jones at forward; Cheeks, Doug Collins, and Andrew Toney at

The unselfish Bobby Jones.

guard; and Caldwell Jones and Darryl Dawkins at center—were incredible. They won with great consistency during the regular season, yet they always seemed to come up short in the NBA playoffs. The Sixers needed one additional quality performer who could put them over the top, a "Moses" to lead them to the promised land.

MOSES MALONE MAKES THE DIFFERENCE

Billy Cunningham found his Moses starring in Houston for the Rockets. After averaging 23.9 points a game and 1,100 rebounds a season during six years with the Rockets, and winning two MVP awards, Moses Malone was traded to the Sixers for Caldwell Jones and millions of dollars. Although Malone seemed to be the dominant player the 76ers needed, many people believed that he could not share the spotlight with Julius Erving.

But the Doctor put a stop to such thoughts. "There are more important things than being a star," Erving said firmly. "At this point, winning the title is the only thing that's on my mind, and there's no question that Moses can help get us there. He's the hardest-working player in the league and just supreme in the pivot. I'm proud to be playing at his side."

Side by side, Erving and Malone powered the Sixers to 65 victories during the 1982–83 season and finally to an NBA championship. Malone was named MVP for both the regular season and the playoffs. But Erving was the happiest of all. "We've been trying to get this for seven years," he said, hoisting the NBA trophy high above his head. "This isn't the end of a long, cumbersome journey—this is the beginning."

1 9 7 9

Maurice Cheeks led the club in assists (431) for the first of 11 seasons in a row.

Andrew Toney sank 25 three-point field goals to lead the team in shots from that range.

But it was not to be. In 1983–84, the Sixers won 13 fewer games than during their championship year, and their season ended with three puzzling losses during the playoffs to the upstart New Jersey Nets. The team that had garnered the NBA crown the year before had lost its edge.

Part of the problem seemed to be age. Many Sixers stars were getting past their prime, which led to changes in this talented cast of characters. The process began at the end of the 1984–85 season, when coach Cunningham decided to resign. He was replaced by his assistant coach, Matt Guokas.

The next to go was Moses Malone, whose constant demands for more money finally led to his being traded to the Washington Bullets following the 1985–86 season. After the next year, Julius Erving left too, deciding to retire because he could no longer perform as consistently as he desired.

Erving's retirement threw the club into a bit of a tailspin. The Sixers had a losing record (36–46) in 1987–88 and failed to make the playoffs for the first time in 13 seasons.

Still, things were not so bleak in Philadelphia. The club still had Maurice Cheeks, as well as a one-man wrecking crew named Charles Barkley, one of the NBA's most unusual and exciting stars.

DON'T MAKE CHARLES MAD

When Charles Barkley arrived in the NBA at the start of the 1984–85 season, no one knew exactly what to expect from him. He wasn't very tall, he didn't jump very well, and he seemed a little too overweight to become an NBA star. The 6-foot-5, 280-pound Barkley, who came out of

Auburn University, was nicknamed "the round mound of re-bound." But he was fierce on the court. Barkley immediately established himself as a ferocious competitor who some-times lost control in the heat of battle; for several seasons, he led the league in technical fouls. But he also drove his teammates to work as hard as he did on the floor. "Charles gets us awake at times," Maurice Cheeks said. "We some-times get on too low a flame, but then Charles comes along and tears down the backboard or something, and we re-member what we're out there for. We'd better. We don't want Charles to be mad at us."

In his first year as a 76er, rookie Hersey Hawkins averaged 15.1 points a game.

Mad or not, Charles Barkley quickly made his mark in Philadelphia, and when Julius Erving retired, he became the club's unquestioned leader. He was named to the first team All-NBA squad for four straight seasons from 1987–88 to 1991–92, and quickly rose in club rankings in scoring, offen-sive and defensive rebounding, free-throw shooting, and minutes played.

Unfortunately, Barkley could not make the Sixers big win-ners all by himself. The club also needed better talent in the backcourt and on the boards. Guards Hersey Hawkins and Johnny Dawkins provided a spark with their scoring and ball handling, and frontcourt men Armon Gilliam and Manute Bol, a 7-foot-7 former tribesman from Sudan, added re-bounding support. But they were not enough. The 76ers were slowly overtaken by other teams in the league, and the club's record drifted below .500.

The losing frustrated Charles Barkley. He asked to be traded to a team with a better chance of winning an NBA championship soon, and the 76ers granted his request. He

Charles Barkley, a 76ers scoring leader (pages 26–27).

*In his first season
in Philadelphia,
Manute Bol set a
club record with
205 blocked shots.*

was sent to the Phoenix Suns before the 1992-93 season in exchange for All-Star guard Jeff Hornacek and two young frontcourt players, Tim Perry and Andrew Lang. "I want to be in 'The Big Show' [the NBA finals] just once," Barkley explained to Philadelphia's disappointed fans.

Barkley got his chance the next season when he led the Suns all the way to the NBA finals against Michael Jordan and the Chicago Bulls. Meanwhile the 76ers fell futher into the league cellar.

The one highlight for the club during the early 1990s was the play of forward Clarence Weatherspoon, an explosive forward from Southern Mississippi University, whose build and power on the court reminded many fans of Charles Barkley. "Spoon" was the 76ers' first-round draft pick in 1992, and he quickly became a fan favorite.

Unfortunately the club's top draft pick the next season didn't fare as well. Big things were expected of 1993 first-rounder Shawn Bradley. After all, at 7-foot-6, he was truly big. But Bradley, who had played only one season at Brigham Young University before spending two years as a Mormon missionary in Australia, lacked experience and body strength to compete with the more powerful centers in the league. He was a great shot-blocker but was not the rebounder or scorer that club management hoped he would be. Philadelphia fans booed Bradley mercilessly, and the gentle big man quickly lost confidence in his ability. Finally, the team gave up on Bradley and traded him to New Jersey for Derrick Coleman, a former All-Star whose value had fallen because of injuries and attitude problems.

Meanwhile, the team continued its floundering. The 76ers

had five straight losing seasons between 1991–92 and 1995–96 and became the first NBA team in history to have its record get worse six years in a row. That was the "bad news." The "good news" was that low finishes in the standings meant that Philadelphia would get high picks in the college draft. Team management put those picks to great use in 1995 and 1996 and began building the 76ers team of the future.

1 9 9 3

All-Star guard Jeff Hornacek dropped in 97 three-point shots for the season.

BUILDING FOR THE NEW CENTURY

Holding the hopes of Philadelphia fans in their hands are two outstanding ball handlers and scorers, Jerry Stackhouse and Allen Iverson. The two men don't look or play alike, but they do complement each other nicely.

Stackhouse, Philly's first-round pick in 1995 out of North Carolina, is a tall guard, at 6-foot-6, who plays fiercely on the court but is gentle off of it. He was raised to be humble and peaceful by his mother, the Reverend Minnie Pernell Stackhouse. He lets his play and not his mouth do the talking for him, and his slashing moves and powerful dunks say plenty. "It's been a long time since I've seen somebody as naturally talented as Jerry," says teammate Michael Cage, who has seen lots of players in his 12-year NBA career. "When he goes to the basket and gets the crowd rocking and rolling, that picks us all up."

Stackhouse may have gotten things rolling in 1995–96, but the ground has been shaking in Philadelphia since 20-year-old backcourt mate Allen Iverson arrived from Georgetown as the number one pick in the 1996 college draft. Iverson is six inches shorter than Stackhouse and is far from quiet or

Rookie of the Year Allen Iverson.

Jerry Stackhouse, a fine all-around player.

Derrick Coleman joined the 76ers as the NCAA's all-time top rebounder (1,537) and top scorer (2,143).

gentle. In fact, some NBA veterans feel that the newcomer has been downright disrespectful to his elders in the league. They may not like his attitude, but they have to admire his talent. Voted the 1996–97 Rookie of the Year, everyone agrees that Iverson is not only incredibly fast, but he's powerful at tearing down defenses.

"I try to put pressure on the defense, try to create things for my teammates and myself. I am always, always looking to score, always looking to try to make something happen on the court," Iverson explains.

Stackhouse and Iverson are great talents individually, and the Philadelphia club is hopeful that they can become a real force together. The backcourt duo is the heart of the revitalized 76ers, but Derrick Coleman, Clarence Weatherspoon, and Scott Williams are also an important ingredient in leading the franchise back to the top of the NBA standings.

The club is looking to revitalize its front office also. After posting the third-worst mark in franchise history, general manager Brad Greenburg and head coach Johnny Davis were fired. It was then announced that former Pacers coach Larry Brown would take the helm in Philadelphia beginning with the 1997–98 season.

Leadership and roster changes may have thrown a few wrenches into the gears, but Philadelphia fans can be sure that under Brown's guidance there will be some serious building going on in the "nation's hero factory."